Kleidung
Veshjet

Deutsch-Albanisch

Zweisprachiges Bildwörterbuch für Kinder

Von Richard Carlson Jr.

© copyright 2017 Richard Carlson Jr.
illustrations © copyright 2004-2014 Nova Development and its licensors

Professional human translations by OneHourTranslation.com

All rights reserved.

The author would like to thank the translators for their help.

Hut
kapele

Schal
shall

Handschuhe
dorashka

Mantel

pallto

Mütze
kapele

Socken
çorape

Sneakers
atlete

T-Shirt
bluzë me mëngë të shkurtra

Sweatshirt
xhup

Gürtel
rrip

Shorts
Pantallona të shkurtra

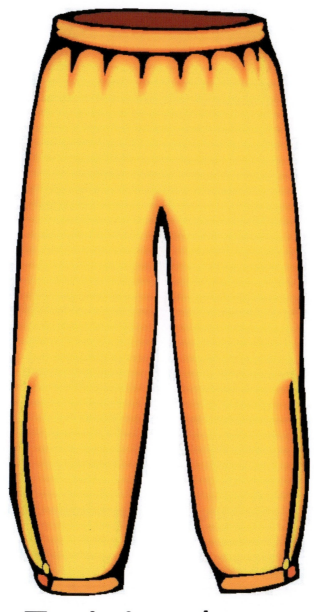

Trainingshose

tuta

Pullover
triko/pulovër

Schuhe
këpucë

Rock
fund

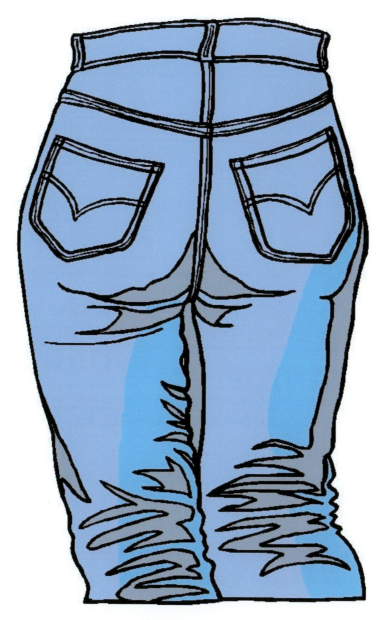

Jeans

xhinse

Bademantel
peshqir

Schlafanzug
pizhame

Hausschuhe
pantofla

Kleid

fustan

Tasche
çantë

Uhr
orë dore

Stiefel
çizme

Hemd
bluze

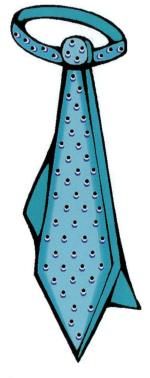

Fliege
papion

Krawatte
kollare

Brille
syze optike

Jacke

xhaketë

Badeanzug
rroba banje

Sonnenbrille
syze dielli

Sandalen
sandale

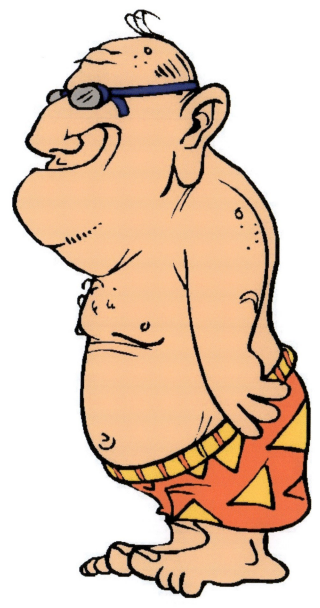

Badehose
rroba banje

Über dieses Buch: Lerne die verschiedenen Kleidungsstücke mit diesem zweisprachigen Bildwörterbuch für Kinder.

Über den Autor: Richard Carlson Jr. ist ein Autor zweisprachiger Kinderbücher. www.rich.center.

Printed in Germany
by Amazon Distribution
GmbH, Leipzig